Theodore Roosevelt

and the Exploration of the Amazon Basin

Explorers of New Worlds

Theodore Roosevelt

and the Exploration
of the Amazon Basin

Richard Kozar

Chelsea House Publishers
Philadelphia

Prepared for Chelsea House Publishers by:
OTTN Publishing, Stockton, N.J.

CHELSEA HOUSE PUBLISHERS
Production Manager: Pamela Loos
Art Director: Sara Davis
Director of Photography: Judy L. Hasday
Managing Editor: James D. Gallagher
Senior Production Editor: J. Christopher Higgins
Series Designer: Keith Trego
Cover Design: Forman Group

First Printing
1 3 5 7 9 8 6 4 2

Library of Congress Cataloging-in-Publication Data

Kozar, Richard.
  Theodore Roosevelt and the exploration of the
    Amazon basin / Richard Kozar.
      p.   cm. – (Explorers of new worlds)
Includes bibliographical references and index.
ISBN 0-7910-5954-5 (hc) – ISBN 0-7910-6164-7 (pbk.)
1. Amazon River Valley–Description and travel–Juve-
nile literature. 2. Natural history–Amazon River
Valley–Juvenile literature. 3. Roosevelt-Rondon
cientific Expedition (1913-1914)–Juvenile literature.
4. Roosevelt, Theodore, 1858-1919–Journeys–Brazil–
Amazon River Valley–Juvenile literature. [1. Roosevelt,
Theodore, 1858-1919. 2. Presidents. 3. Explorers.
4. Roosevelt-Rondon Scientific Expedition (1913-1914).
5. Amazon River Valley–Description and travel.]
I. Title. II. Series.

F2546.K79 2000
918.1'1045–dc21
                                                    00-034596

Contents

The Razor's
Edge

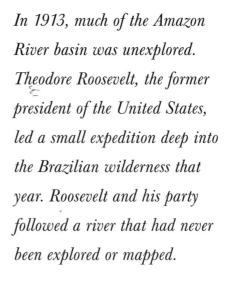

In 1913, much of the Amazon River basin was unexplored. Theodore Roosevelt, the former president of the United States, led a small expedition deep into the Brazilian wilderness that year. Roosevelt and his party followed a river that had never been explored or mapped.

I

𝐼 magine yourself smack in the middle of the steamy Amazon rain forest, where everything conspires against your survival: wilting heat, incessant rain showers, perilous river rapids, biting bugs, man-eating fish, poisonous snakes, and tropical fevers. Who in his right mind would ever seek out such a nightmarish place? America's 26th president, Theodore Roosevelt, for one, and he did it back in 1913, when much of the Brazilian tropics was still

Theodore Roosevelt was an avid hunter and outdoorsman. After leaving the White House in 1908, he traveled to Africa to hunt big game. In 1912, he made a bid to return to the White House, but was defeated; the next year, he decided to travel through the Amazon rain forest.

unexplored wilderness. But for Roosevelt, who had already served out his two terms as president, the chance to be the first to explore remote frontier–regardless of the danger–was too good to pass up.

Such bravado was vintage Roosevelt. If ever there was a man who lived on the razor's edge, who exulted in the face of danger and death, it was he. His hazardous journey through the Amazon region was just one of a string of adventures to the wilds he made in his life. Trips to the most remote regions of the American west, Africa, and India were already under his belt, so he was familiar with wild animals like grizzly bears, charging rhinos, and venom-spitting cobras. But even he wasn't quite prepared for *piranhas*–fish that could strip the flesh off a live cow in minutes–or deadly tropical pit vipers that could kill a man with one bite. And there were ants and termites that could eat a man's clothing into tatters overnight.

Nonetheless, Roosevelt marveled at the awesome beauty of the Amazon region. The rain forest was a virgin region in those early days of the 20th century, home to exotic tropical flowers, birds, fish, and mammals, many of which had never even been documented.

Part of the path Roosevelt chose to take on his Brazilian adventure had never been traveled by a white man. The river system he intended to explore did not show up on any maps, nor was anyone even certain how far it ran or where it ended. But if Roosevelt had any qualms about proceeding, he never voiced them. He wasn't about to live a quiet life, regardless of the risks. He once wrote, "Only those are fit to live who do not fear to die; and none are fit to die who have shrunk from the joy of life and the duty of life. Both life and death are part of the same Great Adventure."

Strong words from a bear of a man, one whose early life gave no indication of the vigorous adult he would become. In fact, young Theodore was a shy, sickly lad who made his parents wonder if he would live long enough to reach adulthood. As a boy, he was stricken with **asthma**, a medical condition that induces violent coughing and tightness in the chest. Sufferers typically have great difficulty breathing, which can cause them to panic and make their attacks even more severe.

Roosevelt was also a bookworm, and so anxious he imagined all sorts of calamities. This was noteworthy because his own father was naturally outgoing, bold, and in many ways larger than life. Indeed, young Theodore worshipped his dad; it was thanks to his persistence and inspiration that the timid boy gradually transformed into a rugged daredevil who was afraid of no challenge or man—except his father.

This attitude would serve Theodore Roosevelt well in life. The truth is, he probably couldn't have accomplished nearly as much if he hadn't evolved into the "bull in a china shop" he came to be. "Bull" is a good word to describe the grown man, whose favorite expression of approval was "Bully!" Several Roosevelt contemporaries saw him in a similar vein:

Roosevelt, head down, contemplates several boars shot along the Amazon. With him is Colonel Rondon, a Brazilian who accompanied the expedition.

Buffalo Bill Cody called him "a cyclone," and humorist Mark Twain, no big fan, described him as "an earthquake."

Others saw a perennial child in Theodore Roosevelt. Biographer Henry F. Pringle said the "Theodore Roosevelt of later years was the most adolescent of men." And close friend Cecil Spring Rice wrote in 1904: "You must always remember that the President is about six."

He certainly was boyish at times. But most average Americans found him a breath of fresh air—what you saw was what you got. A New York City reporter once had this to say while Roosevelt was fighting corruption as a police commissioner: "He has what is essentially a boy's mind. What he thinks he says at once. . . . It is his distinguishing characteristic. However, with it he has great qualities which make him an invaluable public servant—inflexible honesty, absolute fearlessness, and devotion to good government which amounts to religion."

Americans were fond of calling their headstrong leader "Teddy," a nickname he despised (even though his own family had affectionately called him Teedie as a youngster). The name became more popular than ever after a famous newspaper cartoonist drew a picture of Roosevelt sparing a bear cub's life while hunting in Mississippi. (Actually, the president had refused to shoot an old blind bear his associates had tied up to a tree for him.)

> **One creative toymaker decided to capitalize on the publicity surrounding Roosevelt's Mississippi hunting trip, and introduced a toy that would become famous: the Teddy bear.**

There is much more to Theodore Roosevelt's legacy than stuffed animals, however. He was a fearless defender of American interests, one who fervently felt the nation couldn't bury its head beneath the sand when world events threatened those interests. He had also made it his mission to root out corruption in politics and government, and didn't shy away from attacking big business when he felt it had grown too big for the public good. And last, as president he was America's premier *conservationist*. Roosevelt's love for all things in nature compelled him to study and collect wildlife across the globe, as well as protect vast tracts of America as scenic monuments and national parks, an endowment we enjoy to this day.

As a child, Theodore Roosevelt was not very healthy. His father, whom he loved and admired, encouraged him to build himself both physically and mentally.

From a Tiny Acorn... 2

heodore Roosevelt was born in New York on October 27, 1858, three years before the outbreak of the American Civil War. He was the second of four children born to Theodore and Martha Bullock Roosevelt, a couple whose backgrounds and personalities shaped their marriage as well as their children. Theodore Roosevelt Sr. had descended from Dutch settlers in 17th-century New York. Two centuries after his ancestors had staked a claim in America, the Roosevelts were prosperous glass importers in New York, and among the city's 10 wealthiest families. Martha "Mittie" Bullock, on the other hand, was a Southern belle whose family hailed from Georgia. Her family's interests and values were completely different from those north of the Mason-Dixon line in the 1860s, when the Southern states seceded from the Union rather than give up their slaves. Mittie was also not as outgoing as her prominent husband, but remained a devoted mother to Anna ("Bamie"), Theodore, Elliott, and Corinne.

Though several of the Roosevelt children had poor health, young Theodore was arguably the most sickly. At age three, he began suffering from bouts of asthma, a swelling of the bronchial membranes that can severely restrict breathing. There is medication available today to reduce the symptoms, but still no known cause or cure. Back in the 1860s, asthma attacks must have been as terrifying for Roosevelt's parents as for him.

His bouts literally dictated the entire family's plans on occasion; his mother once turned around on a trip and returned with Theodore because of an onset of the illness. And there are tales of the strong father carrying his frail son for hours throughout their house while he gasped for air, or whisking him into a carriage late at night and racing through Central Park so that air would rush into his lungs.

For a man who claimed to fear little as a grown-up, Theodore was surprisingly timid and nervous as a lad. There was a period, for instance, when he was convinced a werewolf lurked beneath his bed and was going to spring at him in the darkness. He was even afraid to go to church. Moreover, because he and his brother and sisters were not sent to public school, they had few friends outside of Roosevelt cousins.

Thus restricted to a sheltered life, Theodore often turned to reading for comfort. He preferred the serene world of nature to boisterous activity. For

> **Theodore's eyesight was weak, and progressively worsened as he grew older, especially after a White House boxing session during which he was punched in the eye. By 1908, as his presidential term was ending, he lost sight in his left eye altogether, a closely kept secret.**

example, he became a "naturalist" at age seven, and demonstrated his love for birds and insects by co-founding "The Roosevelt Museum of Natural History" with two cousins. Among its first acquisitions were a seal's skull and assorted bugs and small mammals.

Theodore was so fascinated with animals that he

learned **taxidermy**, the art of preserving and mounting animal skins. His work was made considerably easier when his father gave him his first gun at age 14 so he could collect animals and birds himself. His parents' attic became the museum, and he rapidly filled it with specimens from near and far, including several birds collected on a visit to Egypt. His parents also purchased his first set of eyeglasses, which truly expanded his horizons. "I had no idea how beautiful the world was until I got those spectacles," he later said.

Indeed, thanks to his patient, understanding parents, the man who would lead a charge up San Juan Hill several decades later eventually grew out of his childhood fears and frailties. The turning point may have been a firm talk from his father following a year-long trip to Europe. "You have the mind but not the body," Theodore Sr. told his son, "and without the help of the body the mind cannot go as far as it should. You must make your body." The young lad took his father's advice to heart and somewhat reluctantly embarked on a fitness regimen of weight lifting and rigorous activity for the next two years.

But exercise took on a whole new meaning after Theodore was embarrassed to learn he couldn't protect himself against four taunting teens on a stage-coach ride to Maine. He was defenseless against the weakest of the bullies. That convinced him to take up the gentlemen's sport of boxing, and before long he wrote in his diary that he was giving as well as receiving black eyes. He also learned how to ride horses, a skill he would use later in life.

The elder Roosevelt was unquestionably the strongest influence on young Theodore, who considered him the finest man he had ever known. Not only was his dad a devoted father, he was also a respected businessman and philanthropist who dedicated his life and resources to helping those in need. Children who knew him followed him like the Pied Piper.

One of the few disagreements between the two Theodores came after war broke out between the North and South in 1861. The elder Roosevelt chose not to fight out of respect for his wife, whose own brothers and relatives had all joined the Confederate Army. At the time, a man could avoid serving in the Union military by literally paying someone else to take his place, which Theodore Sr.—like many other well-to-do Northerners, including all the eligible men in his family—chose to do.

*The Civil War was one of the few subjects on which
Theodore disagreed with his father. The elder Roosevelt
had opted not to fight in the war; historians believe his
son never understood this decision.*

Young Theodore, however, full of boyish pride
and Union patriotism, was overheard by his Aunt
Anna one night during his prayers asking God to
"grind the Southern troops to powder." Many have
speculated that the boy never understood his

father's decision not to fight, and consequently spent his whole life searching for opportunities to prove his own gallantry.

By 1876, Theodore was growing from a skinny teen into a strapping youth. His athletic skill broadened as well, especially in track. Befitting his family's prominence, he applied to and was accepted at Harvard University in Boston, a prestigious school. And his love affair with things natural continued; the summer following his freshman year he and a friend trooped off to the Adirondack Mountains on a birdwatching excursion and later published a book called *The Summer Birds of the Adirondacks.*

A year later, however, young Theodore suffered a terrible blow when his 46-year-old father died from cancer on February 9, 1877. "I felt as if I had been stunned, or as if part of my life had been taken away," he said. "He was everything to me."

Copyright 1898
by B. J. Fall

Lieutenant Colonel Theodore Roosevelt in his uniform as a Rough Rider. Roosevelt gained national fame during the Spanish-American War in 1898.

Coming of Age

3

There is some debate as to how much Theodore learned while at Harvard, but this much is certain: he was maturing physically and becoming more confident in his own skin. He had become a campus character, suddenly concerned with how he dressed as he dashed from one activity to the next. He joined the rifle club, glee club, finance club, Harvard's most elite social club, and the school newspaper. Moreover, he fell head over heels in love with 17-year-old Alice Hathaway Lee, a sweet, shy girl who came from a prominent Boston family.

Initially she resisted his enthusiastic courtship attempts,

and turned down his first proposal of marriage. But Alice ultimately succumbed to the persistent New Yorker. They were married on his 22nd birthday, October 27, 1880, several months after Theodore graduated from Harvard.

The Roosevelts spent three happy but whirlwind years together, as Theodore lurched from one pre-occupation to the next. He spent a year attending Columbia University Law School, but grew bored with law and never completed his studies. Instead, he was persuaded to run for a seat in the New York legislature, despite the low regard people of his class held for politics. He won his first election, and went on to win two more one-year terms.

On February 13, 1884, Theodore was working at the state capital in Albany when word reached him that Alice had given birth to a baby girl, who was named after her. Although his wife had not been the picture of health throughout her first pregnancy, everything appeared to have gone well. Theodore headed home to celebrate the occasion, only to be met at the front door of the family house by his brother Elliott, who delivered the devastating news: "There is a curse on this house! Mother is dying and Alice is dying too."

Early the following day, Mittie Roosevelt died of a sudden onset of typhoid fever, and by 2 P.M., Alice Roosevelt slipped away after suffering from complications of Bright's disease, an inflammation of the kidneys. Theodore managed to write in his diary that night, "The light has gone out of my life."

He nonetheless returned to complete his final term in the legislature, which ended that spring. Meanwhile, he left his infant daughter in the care of his sister Bamie.

After the legislative session ended, Roosevelt headed out west to the Badlands in what is now North Dakota. There he bought two cattle ranches and decided to live the life of a cowboy while he debated what trail to follow next in life.

However colorful cattle ranching could be, it was not Roosevelt's ultimate calling. In fact, after the brutal winter of 1886–87, most of his herd died. Theodore was forced to sell his remaining animals and land for far less than he had invested in them.

He subsequently returned to New York City, where he agreed to run for the office of mayor. Roosevelt thought his chance of winning was slim, and indeed, he lost. But his personal life was once again on an upswing. On December 6, 1886, he married

a

A Roosevelt family portrait. From left to right are
Quentin, Theodore Roosevelt, Theodore III, Archibald,
Alice, Kermit, Edith Carow Roosevelt, and Ethel.

childhood sweetheart, Edith Carow, who would become the kind of strong lifelong partner essential to a man like Roosevelt. Together they would have five children of their own: Theodore III, born in 1887; Kermit, 1889; Ethel, 1891; Archibald, 1894; and Quentin in 1897.

Theodore Roosevelt's own children brought out the boy trapped inside him, the adolescent side so many of his associates would tease him about after he became president. Edith and her husband also built a 22-room house on Long Island and named it Sagamore Hill. Primarily built as a summer house, it nonetheless became the center of the Roosevelt clan's boisterous family life, and would serve as a country retreat for decades to come, much as Hyannisport, Massachusetts, became synonymous with the Kennedys.

Politics continued to attract Theodore like a moth to a flame. After supporting Republican presidential candidate Benjamin Harrison in his successful 1889 campaign, Roosevelt won an appointment to the Civil Service Commission. The job was hardly a plum assignment. As commissioner, Roosevelt was supposed to ensure that government jobs were given to the most qualified people. Previously, whichever political party was in power had given jobs to their campaign supporters or to friends and family members. Roosevelt enforced fair-hiring practices, even though this gained him more enemies than friends in both parties.

His next post, as president of the Board of Police Commissioners in New York City, gave him the same ***bully pulpit*** from which he could root out corruption in the city's police force. At the time, getting promotions and plum assignments in the police force often meant paying some official for the privilege. This practice, which fostered a system of bribery and police payoffs, disgusted Roosevelt. For several years he fought for a system that awarded promotions on merit rather than bribery. He even took to walking the city streets at night to ensure policemen were patrolling rather than loafing in a squad room.

Roosevelt's reputation as a reformer made him very well known. In 1896 he campaigned on behalf of Republican William McKinley, who was seeking the presidency. The Republican candidate won, and in gratitude for Roosevelt's support McKinley appointed him assistant secretary of the navy.

Theodore felt right at home working for the navy. After all, he had written a highly regarded book, *The Naval War of 1812*, earlier in his career. Roosevelt fully intended to use his powerful new position to lobby for a stronger naval force. In his opinion, the U.S. Navy had fallen into disrepair after the end of the Civil War.

Roosevelt had grave doubts about the ability of the United States to defend its interests around the

An illustration depicts the battleship Maine *exploding in Havana harbor. While even today the cause of the explosion is unknown, anti-Spanish sentiment at the time caused President McKinley to declare war.*

world. One example of this was neighboring Cuba, whose citizens had long chafed under Spanish rule and were in open revolt. Most Americans favored freedom for Cuba.

A tense situation occurred when the U.S. battleship *Maine*, anchored just outside Havana harbor, blew up on February 15, 1898, killing 262 American

*In this idealized painting, Roosevelt leads the Rough
Riders up San Juan Hill. His exploits during the
Spanish-American War made Roosevelt one of the
most famous men in America.*

sailors. Though even today no one knows exactly
what caused the explosion (it might actually have
been triggered accidentally by the ship's crew), the
American press urged retaliation against the Spanish. The U.S. declared war on Spain on April 25,
thus igniting the Spanish-American War.

The war provided Roosevelt, always something of a glory hound, a perfect opportunity to prove himself in battle. He immediately resigned his naval position and joined the army, where he was given the rank of lieutenant colonel in the First Volunteer Cavalry Regiment. Before long, however, the regiment would become known as Roosevelt's Rough Riders, even though Theodore wasn't even its commanding officer.

Roosevelt's day in the sun finally came on July 1, 1898, when he dodged a hail of bullets while leading a charge in the battle of San Juan Hill. Roosevelt reveled in his ultimate victory, despite losing 66 of his men during the assault up what was called Kettle Hill. In fact, a few observers at the time and several since have questioned the wisdom of his famous charge altogether. Nevertheless, Roosevelt came home from Cuba a war hero. This fame helped sweep him into the New York State governor's mansion in the election that year.

Roosevelt, shown here delivering a speech, was considered an excellent candidate to be William McKinley's vice president in the 1900 election.

White House Bound

4

By 1900, Roosevelt's name was being tossed about as a vice-presidential running mate of President William McKinley, who was running for a second term. Although Theodore cringed at the thought of holding what was a purely ceremonial job at the time, he agreed to accept his party's nomination. Afterward, he threw himself into the campaign, making hundreds of speeches across the country. His work paid off. In 1901 he and McKinley were sworn in as president and vice president.

Roosevelt fully expected to spend the next four years doing little but biding his time until the next presidential

William McKinley was elected to a second term as president in 1900, but early in the term he was shot and killed. His vice president, Theodore Roosevelt, was sworn in as president on September 14, 1901.

election, but once again fate intervened. In September 1901 McKinley was shot by an assassin while attending the Pan American Exposition in Buffalo, New York. Although initially expected to recover, he died nine days afterward. Theodore Roosevelt was sworn in as the country's 26th president on September 14, 1901. At age 42, he was the youngest man ever to become president.

Although he would have preferred to enter the Oval Office on his own merits, Roosevelt "seized the bull by the horns." Relying on a familiar theme, he set his sights on what he felt were the corrupting practices of big business. At the time, corporations often formed trusts under which they agreed not to undercut each other by charging lower prices for their product, whether it be steel or oil. Consumers usually lost out because they then had to pay higher prices. Although trusts had been outlawed for over a decade, Roosevelt was the first president to actively enforce the law, helping break up some of the biggest corporate trusts in America during his administration.

He was also no stranger to foreign affairs, particularly in South America. His biggest accomplishment there was reaching an agreement with government officials in the Isthmus of Panama to build the Panama Canal. Although scores of workers died from malaria over the nine years the 50-mile canal took to build, the engineering marvel guaranteed America quick access to the Pacific Ocean for both its merchant and war ships.

Despite Roosevelt's achievements after succeeding McKinley, he wondered whether he could win a presidential election in his own right. In 1904, however, an adoring public inspired by his colorful leadership overwhelmingly elected him.

Theodore Roosevelt became America's most

conservation-minded president. He saw to it that 230 million acres of American forest, desert, and plains became federal land, protected from unregulated development. Included in that number were several national parks, 50 national wildlife refuges, and the first 18 national monuments.

In addition, he was a superb international statesman. Because of his success negotiating an end to war between Russia and Japan, Roosevelt was awarded the Nobel Peace Prize in 1906, the first American thus honored.

As President Roosevelt had promised, he did not run for another four-year term in 1908. Instead, he backed William Howard Taft, his secretary of war, who easily defeated the Democratic nominee.

Roosevelt vowed to stay out of politics after his departure from Washington, but it proved to be a far easier promise to make than uphold over the next decade. He at least tried to pursue other interests. Two weeks after quietly leaving Washington, D.C., he went on *safari* to Africa, where he collected scores of big-game animals for the Museum of Natural History in New York, which his father had cofounded.

And four years later, he decided to go exploring

Theodore Roosevelt loved the challenge of big-game hunting. After leaving the White House, he went on safari to Africa. He shot this jaguar while journeying through the Brazilian wilderness in 1913.

once again with Father Zahm, a friend who had first invited him in 1908 to join an expedition through the Amazon Valley of South America. This time, after accepting invitations from officials in Argentina and Brazil to lecture over a six-week period, Roosevelt signed on.

In typical fashion, he decided to combine a working trip with adventure, and convinced the directors of the American Museum of Natural History in New York to sponsor and staff the trip. Originally, it was to study birds and mammals. But the expedition turned out to be far more expansive in scope.

Joining him were bird specialist George K. Cherrie, and Leo E. Miller, who studied mammals. Both were well acquainted with tropical forests. Also joining the team were Roosevelt's son Kermit, along with Father Zahm. They were to be joined by Colonel Candido Mariano da Silva Rondon, a legendary Brazilian army explorer who was Indian by descent. He had surveyed much of Brazil for telegraph lines and railroads, and later built 3,000 miles of telegraph.

Fully intending to collect exotic "specimens" for the museum during the Amazon trip, Roosevelt naturally brought a small arsenal with him, including shotguns, rifles, and pistols. The group also outfitted themselves in New York with tents, cots, mosquito nets, and assorted canned foods, which they would rely on to supplement the wild game and fish they hoped would provide most of the food.

The Americans were embarking on a difficult journey to the largest river basin in the world, home to countless insects, reptiles, and animals that would just as soon take a bite out of a man as any other local food source. Moreover, because of the tropical heat and heavy rainfall, navigating through such forests was a challenge for local natives, let alone white men who were unfamiliar with traveling such challenging terrain.

They intended to start the trip in Paraguay, heading up the Paraguay River to the headwaters of the Amazon.

The Adventure Begins

Explorers of New Worlds

Roosevelt started his exploration of the Amazon River basin with a riverboat ride provided by the president of Paraguay. Soon, the explorers would find themselves traveling through the wilderness much less comfortably—first walking through the jungle with a mule train, and later in small canoes.

5

oosevelt joined his fellow explorers in the city of Asunción, Paraguay, where they headed up the river in style—in the personal steamer-gunboat of the country's president (with the American flag on its mast). For at least the start of the voyage, the food was plentiful and tasty, the insects no problem, and the scenery and animal life spectacular. Roosevelt was particularly taken with the bird life: "crimson flamingoes and rosy spoonbills, dark-colored ibis and white storks with black wings. Darters, with snakelike necks and pointed bills, perched in the trees on the brink of the river. Snow egrets flapped across the marshes."

Although the Paraguay River seemed to act as a barrier to both mosquitoes and sand-flies, Cherrie and Miller warned Roosevelt how miserable they had been while awaiting his arrival on a vast grassland beyond the river. The former president duly noted their woes in his trusty diary: "The sand-flies crawled through the meshes in the mosquito-nets, and forbade them to sleep; if in their sleep a knee touched the net the mosquitoes fell on it so that it looked as if riddled by birdshot. . . ."

Roosevelt soon encountered another dreaded denizen of the Amazon basin—the piranha, which he called the "most ferocious fish in the world." He noted that they reached a length of nearly 18 inches and were easily caught in the waters of the river. However, piranhas "habitually attack things much larger than themselves," he said. "They will snap a finger off a hand incautiously trailed in the water; they mutilate swimmers—in every river town in Paraguay there are men who have thus been mutilated; they will rend and devour alive any wounded man or beast; for blood in the water excites them to madness." He added that piranhas were also capable of biting through fishhooks and the wire used as leaders. "The head with its short muzzle, staring malignant eyes, and gaping, cruelly armed jaws, is the embodiment of evil ferocity; and the actions of the fish exactly match its looks."

He did find the people exceptionally warm and welcoming to foreign dignitaries such as he, particularly when he was invited by officials in the town of Concepción to a reception. It was a grand affair, he recalled, noting that the locals were customarily dressed far more formally than the Americans and were generally more gracious.

Shortly after crossing the Brazilian border, the expedition was joined by Colonel Rondon and his associates. Roosevelt quickly hit it off with the Brazilian tamer of the wilderness, who told story upon story about piranha attacks and deadly snakes. Rondon said they all paled, however, in comparison to the real danger of the tropics–insects. Roosevelt agreed, saying, "In these forests the multitude of insects that bite, sting, devour, and prey upon other creatures, often with accompaniments of atrocious suffering, passes belief."

And he seldom passed up the chance to mention how wild the region remained, even though parts of it were already colonized and fairly well traveled. "The work done by the original explorers of such a wilderness necessitates the undergoing of untold hardship and danger. Their successors, even their immediate successors, have a relatively easy time," Roosevelt wrote. "Soon the road becomes so well beaten that it can be traversed without hardship by any man who does not venture from it—although if he goes off into the wilderness for even one day, hunting or collecting, he will have a slight taste of what his predecessors endured. The wilderness explored by Colonel Rondon is not yet wholly sub-dued, and still holds menace to human life."

Indeed, one of Rondon's best men, a Captain Cardozo, died of **beriberi**, a tropical disease, while scouting the wilderness for Roosevelt's party. And three more of his workers died when their riverboat overturned, drowning them and losing all of their **provisions**. To undertake such hazards of the wilder-ness, workers had to be paid seven times what they normally earned.

Roosevelt's expedition of 30, now crammed into a houseboat and a small launch, continued upstream. The boats struggled against the rising speed of the current, and the weight of all the necessary provisions and specimens collected so far. Their speed was about a mile and a half per hour. The jungle lining the river rose up like walls, noted Roosevelt: "It was like passing through a gigantic greenhouse." So thick was the overhanging river's-edge canopy that just seeing the bank, let alone climbing up it, was a near impossibility.

Some of the exotic—and dangerous—animals the explorers encountered were meat-eating fish called piranhas, as well as poisonous snakes.

At the town of Tapirapoan, the headquarters of the Telegraphic Commission, the men went ashore to prepare for a difficult stretch of their trip—their journey through the jungle, which would not be a scenic, specimen-gathering jaunt but more of a forced march. Here, while checking his mammal traps one morning, Miller ran into a column of **army ants**: fierce, fast-moving hordes dreaded by animal and man alike. They "move in big bodies and destroy or make prey of every living thing that is unable or unwilling to get out of their path in time," observed Roosevelt, who added that centipedes, spiders, and scorpions, as well as nestling birds, all fell prey to the marauding ants.

He recorded that the heat was between 94 and 104 degrees Fahrenheit, and the air dripping with moisture. At this point, over 1,000 bird and 250 mammal specimens were sent back downstream with several men. They would eventually go to New York for mounting.

The party also split up, with some baggage going on ahead on mules and oxen while the main

> After Roosevelt encountered *vampire bats*, he wrote, "South America makes up for its lack, relatively to Africa and India, of large man-eating carnivores by the extraordinary ferocity or bloodthirstiness of certain small creatures of which the kinsfolk elsewhere are harmless. It is only here that fish no bigger than trout kill swimmers, and bats the size of the ordinary 'flittermice' of the northern hemisphere drain the life-blood of big beasts and of man himself."

group waited to follow into the highland wilderness of Brazil.

On January 21, Roosevelt's mule train left the camp, crossing the flat terrain fairly quickly. He couldn't help commenting on the suitability of the geography for farming and cattle-raising. "It is a fine country for settlement," he said, noting gladly that it was remarkably free of mosquitoes.

Although much of their journey had been plagued by countless biting, stinging pests of one sort or another, Roosevelt said such hardships were to be expected by groundbreakers. "The original explorer, and to an only less degree the hard-working field naturalist or big-game hunter, have to face these pests, just as they have to face countless risks, hardships, and difficulties," he said.

The expedition continued across the high plain, leaving behind the lush tropical jungle and oppressive humidity for a more arid countryside where sleeping actually required blankets for comfort. At one point, Roosevelt's Brazilian hosts provided motorized trucks from the telegraph company to run on ahead of the main party and carry equipment. This gave the tired mules a bit of a break.

On February 27, 1914, the expedition at last

began heading down the Rio Duvida, or River of Doubt (so named because no one had ever explored the length of its course). The men began their descent of the river in seven dugout canoes, with only as much food and ammunition as they felt would be absolutely necessary to maintain their survival. Still, their watercraft were overloaded to the point of swamping. "One was small, one was cranky, and two were old, waterlogged, and leaky," wrote Roosevelt. Adding to their discomforts, the rainy season was also in full swing, swelling the rivers and raising havoc with the equipment. "It was not possible to keep the moisture out of our belongings; everything became mouldy except what became rusty," Roosevelt observed dryly.

Paddling the canoes and performing the grueling work on this leg of the trip were seasoned Brazilian *camaradas*, Roosevelt happily reported. The men "were lithe as panthers and brawny as bears. They swam like water-dogs. They were equally at home with pole and paddle, with axe and machete; and one was a good cook and others were good men around camp."

Because the group planned to map the length and course of the river as they went, progress was

Kermit Roosevelt took this photo of a family of Amazon natives and their dwelling.

slow. The most intriguing thing was that no one in the group–including Colonel Rondon–really knew where the River of Doubt would take them, or how long the journey would be. "We did not know whether we had one hundred or eight hundred kilometres to go, whether the stream would be fairly smooth or whether we would encounter waterfalls, or rapids, or even some big marsh or lake," wrote Theodore Roosevelt. "We had entered a land of unknown possibilities."

Theodore Roosevelt in a light-hearted moment.
One of America's most beloved presidents
almost did not survive his expedition through
the Amazon.

Into the Wilderness 6

he expedition traveled nearly 62 miles during the
first week down the river. However, they had actually come only 31 miles north of their starting point
because the river twisted east and west along its course like
a winding anaconda. Thus, with a limited supply of food
and no known end in sight, it was imperative that the men
proceed as rapidly as possible. That would have been fine,
had they not periodically been blocked by river rapids,
most of which they had to **portage** around. This meant lug-
ging their heavy dugout canoes overland for one or more
miles, with the aid of log rollers, block and tackle, and

sheer willpower. At times, their canoes became so decrepit they either sank outright or were damaged in the portages, forcing the *camaradas* to fell huge trees and carve new ones.

On one occasion, the river took its tolls despite the precautions the team undertook. Roosevelt's own son, Kermit, nearly drowned when he and two *camaradas* in his canoe were swept downstream into a swirling rapid. One of the men disappeared beneath the raging water and was never seen again. Kermit lost his favorite rifle in the confusion and would have lost his life had he not grabbed an overhanging branch near the bank and hung on. "It was a very narrow escape," wrote his father. "Kermit was a great comfort and help to me on the trip; but the fear of some fatal accident befalling him was always a nightmare to me. He was to be married as soon as the trip was over; and it did not seem to me that I could bear to bring bad tidings to his betrothed and to his mother."

Tragedy nearly befell them again in another series of rapids not far downstream. Colonel Rondon's dog was killed by Indians shooting poison arrows while master and canine were scouting the riverbank. Meanwhile, a new canoe sank while being towed through the rapids, and the rope and pulleys so important in a portage were also lost. Hauling heavy canoes over any future portages were thus out of the question, and the men also realized they had too much gear for the space now available. In the first 18 days, the expedition had eaten a third of its food. They had covered nearly 78 miles—but had more than five times that distance left to go.

What the fearless but weary men couldn't know was that the worst rapids were still ahead. When they finally encountered them, the men decided to carry their gear along the banks while several paddlers eased the remaining four canoes through the treacherous water.

The Brazilian group decided to name one small tributary Rio Kermit. Colonel Rondon also held a ceremony among the ragtag group to officially designate the main river as Rio Roosevelt. Despite his initial reluctance to accept such an honor, Roosevelt relented, saying, "I was much touched by their action, and by the ceremony itself."

However, there was no end in sight. At one point, the group entered increasingly hilly terrain, which they could observe from a high point of land

After the length of the Duvida River was explored, the
Brazilian government officially renamed it after
Theodore Roosevelt.

overlooking a long gorge. "It was a view well worth seeing; but, beautiful although the country ahead of us was, its character was such as to promise further hardships, difficulty, and exhausting labor, and especially further delay," said Roosevelt. "And delay was a serious matter to men whose food supply was beginning to run short, whose equipment was reduced to the minimum, who for a month, with the utmost toil, had made very slow progress, and who had no idea of either the distance or the difficulties of the route in front of them."

One month after encountering the uninterrupted series of rapids, the expedition had managed only another 68 miles. The goal now was to finally reach flat land again and therefore make better time. The *camaradas* were understandably doubtful the group would ever reach civilization again alive.

As the journey continued, fever began to overtake various members, including Kermit and Roosevelt himself, who at one point was so sick his companions thought he might die.

But on April 15, salvation finally seemed at hand. The rapids were left behind, and the River of Doubt began flowing smooth and wide, a sure sign the worst was behind them. Furthermore, the men saw signs that rubber-tree harvesters had been up this far, and eventually they came across several makeshift huts the men and their families had occupied. At last, they met a family who told them that the river they were traveling fed into the Aripuanan, whose juncture was about 15 days further away.

In 48 days, the crew had covered 186 miles and survived to report their discovery. Roosevelt

The stress of the expedition boiled over one day when one of the *camaradas,* a strong but lazy fellow named Julio, shot a crewmember who had caught him stealing food. Worried that Julio might seek revenge on the whole group in his tormented state of mind, the expedition decided to leave him behind. He was briefly spotted once, then never seen again.

expressed relief for the entire party. "We had passed the period when there was a chance of peril, of disaster, to the whole expedition," he wrote. "There might be risk ahead to individuals, or some difficulties and annoyances for all of us; but there was no longer the least likelihood of any disaster to the expedition as a whole. We no longer had to face continual anxiety, the need of constant economy with food, the duty of labor with no end in sight, and bitter uncertainty as to the future."

Just the same, the lot of them were in sad shape, battered by rapids, insects, and the occasional mishap. Roosevelt had bruised his leg on a boulder and formed an **abscess**, and his fever still had not broken. Nevertheless, he defiantly pushed down the home stretch to relative civilization. And both he and his American compatriots expressed a strong desire to be back in northern climes, where spring was just breaking winter's grasp.

Finally, after spending two months in canoes (February 27 to April 26) and covering 465 miles, Roosevelt's expedition linked up with a camp at the junction of the Castanho (now Rio Roosevelt) and Aripuanan Rivers established earlier by one of Colonel Rondon's crew. After that, it was but a short, swift trip to the Madeira River and then into the mighty Amazon itself, which at that point was so wide Roosevelt couldn't even see the far bank.

All told, the expedition's naturalists had gathered over 2,500 birds, nearly 500 animals, and assorted reptiles and fishes, some never before seen by modern man. A weary former president summed up the team's accomplishments: "We put upon the map a river some fifteen hundred kilometres [930 miles] in length, of which the upper course was not merely utterly unknown to, but unguessed at by, anybody; while the lower course, although known for years to a few rubbermen, was utterly unknown to cartographers. It is the chief affluent of the Madeira, which is itself the chief affluent of the Amazon."

Roosevelt never fully recovered his health after returning from the Amazon. He died in his sleep on January 6, 1919.

Once back in New York, Roosevelt was a shell of his former self. He had lost 35 pounds, aged beyond his years, and still suffered the lingering effects of tropical fever (as he would the remainder of his life). His weakened condition, however, didn't prevent him from weighing in his views on U.S. affairs thereafter. In fact, world events compelled him to do so.

The United States had finally been drawn into World War I in Europe in July 1917, something he had strongly urged, and although he himself was denied a chance to lead a military force there, his sons Ted, Kermit, Archie, and Quentin did join the military effort. And sadly, Quentin was killed in an air battle behind enemy lines on July 17, 1918. Just under four months later, on November 11, 1918, the war ended.

Theodore Roosevelt himself died peacefully at Sagamore Hill two months later on January 6, 1919, at age 60. He had been in and out of the hospital the previous year for various ailments, yet even his doctors were surprised when he died in his sleep. "Death had to take him sleeping," observed U.S. vice president Thomas Marshall at the time, "for if Roosevelt had been awake, there would have been a fight."

Chronology

1858 Theodore Roosevelt born October 27 in New York City.

1869 Tours Europe with family and collects animal specimens.

1876 Enters Harvard University in Boston.

1880 Graduates from Harvard; marries first wife, Alice Hathaway Lee.

1882 Elected to New York state legislature for first of three terms.

1884 Mother Mittie Roosevelt and wife Alice both die on the same day, February 14.

1886 Loses race for mayor of New York; marries Edith Kermit Carow.

1889 Appointed U.S. Civil Service Commissioner.

1895 Appointed to New York City Board of Police Commissioners.

1897 Appointed assistant secretary of the U.S. Navy.

1898 Quits post as assistant secretary of the navy; joins the U.S. cavalry and leads famous charge up San Juan Hill (actually Kettle Hill) during Spanish-American War.

1899 Elected governor of New York.

1901 Elected vice president of the United States; sworn in as president following William McKinley's assassination.

1904 Elected president for a full four-year term.

1909 Collects big game on African safari.

1912 Bid to recapture presidency fails.

1913 Explores Brazilian wilderness on River of Doubt.

1919 Dies at age 60 at Sagamore Hill, Long Island, New York.

abscess–an infected wound, marked by yellowish fluid (pus) and surrounded by inflamed tissue.

army ants–aggressive tropical ants that prey on insects and spiders.

asthma–a medical condition that is marked by a difficulty breathing, a sense of constriction in the chest, and coughing or gasping.

beriberi–a disease that affects the nerves, digestive system, and heart.

bully pulpit–a prominent public position or political office that provides an opportunity for the holder to expound his or her views.

conservationist–a person who advocates careful preservation and protection of natural resources.

piranhas–small South American fish with very sharp teeth that may attack and inflict dangerous wounds upon humans and large animals.

portage–to carry boats and equipment overland either around an obstacle (such as rapids) or from one body of water to another.

provisions–a stock of food and necessary supplies.

safari–a hunting expedition in Africa.

taxidermy–the art of preparing, stuffing, and mounting the skins of animals.

vampire bats–bats found in Central and South America that feed on the blood of birds and mammals.

Further Reading

Brands, H. W. *T.R.: The Last Romantic.* Boulder, Colo.: Basic Books, 1998.

Fritz, Jean. *Bully for You, Teddy Roosevelt.* New York: G. P. Putnam's Sons, 1991.

Gould, Lewis L. *The Presidency of Theodore Roosevelt.* Lawrence: University Press of Kansas, 1992.

Grant, George E. *Carry a Big Stick: The Uncommon Heroism of Theodore Roosevelt.* Nashville, Tenn.: Cumberland House, 1997.

Markham, Lois. *Theodore Roosevelt.* New York: Chelsea House Publishers, 1985.

McCullough, David. *Mornings on Horseback.* New York: Simon and Schuster, 1981.

Pringle, Henry F. *Theodore Roosevelt.* New York: Harcourt, Brace and World, 1931.

Renehan, Edward J. *The Lion's Pride: Theodore Roosevelt and His Family in Peace and War.* New York: Oxford University Press, 1998.

Roosevelt, Theodore. *Through the Brazilian Wilderness.* New York: Charles Scribner's Sons, 1914.

Picture Credits

RICHARD KOZAR has written biographies of Elizabeth Dole, Hillary Rodham Clinton, and Michael J. Fox, and contributed *Lewis and Clark: Explorers of the Louisiana Purchase* and *Daniel Boone and the Exploration of the Frontier* to Chelsea House's EXPLORERS OF NEW WORLDS series. He lives near Latrobe, Pennsylvania, with his wife, Heidi, and daughters Caty and Macy.